D0864282

The Parable

Rebera Elliott Foston M.D., MPH

Copyright © 1994 Rebera Elliott Foston M.D., MPH
All rights reserved. No part of this book may be
reproduced without written permission.
Library of Congress Catalog Card Number 94-070189
Edited by: Cynthia Elliott Garnett, Ed.D., Erma Elliott
Cover Illustration by: Will Foston, M.D.
Text Illustrations by: Tamber McPike,
Rebera Elliott Foston, M.D., MPH
ISBN: 0-9641709-2-2

Forward

Again, I would like to thank
Almighty God
for continuing to bless me
with the gift of poetry.

In addition to my husband Will Daniel,
my sons, Bryan Edward and Amia Kari,
and the rest of my beautiful family,

I would like to thank
the thousands of teenagers
who continue to touch my life.

In my work with teenagers,
I tell them about a land called,
"Better than Good".

I can take them there one time,
but they have to go back on their own.
My joy is seeing thousands of teenagers
journeying back on their own.

I take them to the edge of Excellence.
I show them my footprints,
and those of my wonderful family.

I carefully explain that they must
make their own "Footprints into Excellence"
The illustrations of "footprints" in this manuscript are
symbolic of the Excellence I want for all teenagers

I dedicate this, my third volume of poetry, to all of the
teenagers who have not given up, even though their
cries are still being lost to the night

Table of Contents

Introduction

Rebera Elliott Foston M.D., MPH has always loved to write poetry. She managed to include some creative writing courses in her studies at Fisk University, but her passion for writing soon became overshadowed by her technical studies. She graduated Magna Cum Laude, Phi Beta Kappa in biology from Fisk. Then she received her medical degree from Meharry Medical College in Nashville, and her Masters Degree in Public Health from the University of North Carolina at Chapel Hill. She became a Board Certified Family Practitioner, with an emphasis in Adolescent Health Care, and received her Postdoctoral Fellowship training in Family Medicine, at Michigan State University, in East Lansing. She was the first woman to serve as the Health Commissioner of the city of Gary, Indiana, the place where she was born and reared.

Her passion for writing poetry reemerged in 1985, shortly after she dedicated her medical practice, the Foston Adolescent Care Center, to "Adolescents Only". In that same year, she created the Foston Adolescent Workshop, Inc. Through the Workshop she has helped over 1600 teenagers feel good about themselves, by giving them the time and latitude to hone their musical, writing, acting, speaking, critical thinking and caring skills. However, it was after she had treated the pain of over 16,000 teenage patients, and their families, she decided to try to capture some of their pain on paper. Already thousands of teenagers have been visibly touched by her poetry. Dr. Foston's first book is entitled "You Don't Live On My Street", her second book is "No Stoppin' Sense".

Her long term goal is to create a home that can house hundreds of teenagers who find themselves not being parented. This home will be called, "Somewhere: There is A Place for Us".

A portion of the proceeds from all of her books, and from all of the projects of the Foston Adolescent Workshop Inc., will be used to make this goal a reality.

Dr. Rebera Elliott Foston would like for you to read and enjoy this manuscript. She hopes, as with her first two books, some poem or passage may touch you, help you, heal you, strengthen you or move you in some way.

Will Daniel Foston, M.D.

Chapter One

"The Marshalling"

The Parade...

Little Children worry
'bout what Mama's gonna buy
and who's gonna say
somethin' else to make them cry

And runnin' from water hoses
to keep from gettin' sprayed
Life ain't nothin' but
a Parade

It has a startin' time
and its for a special reason
It can begin on any day
and be in any season

And the silent music for the
different drummer is played
'Cause Life ain't nothin' but
a Parade...

A Good Deed

On one thing I hope
we are all agreed

To grow knowledge, we
must first plant the seed

We've got to want to learn
with a hunger and a greed

If not, more ignorance
we will surely breed

So chile,
learn how to read!

I must beg you
and I usually don't plead

But this is a message
that you must heed

Or you'll be killing yourself
Like you would cut and bleed

What will you do,
When you got a chile to feed

Chile,
If you can't read?

How can we get
up to speed?

To hold us back,
there will be no need

As a Black race how
can we ever succeed?

As a people we can
never be freed

Chile,
until you can read

How do you expect
one day to lead?

"To Learn All We Can" should
be our motto and our creed

or the Black race will
grow like a weed

Do yourself a favor
and the Black race a good deed

Chile, just learn how to read!!!!!

Have To Run

Mama,
I have to
get up now?
I can't
even see the sun

Mama, why are
you actin'
so mad?
Is it somethin'
that I have done?

Mama,
Where are
we goin'?
Will I
have any fun?

Mama,
can I
take my toys?
All the trophies
that I won?

Mama,
look at that
web a
spider must
have spun!

Mama,
I am so
sleepy my
eyelids
weigh a ton

Mama,
is this all
we have to eat,
just a
hot dog bun?

Mama ,
can I take
my dolls?
Not even
a single one?

Mama,
Why are you
cryin'? Why
are you holdin'
Daddy's gun?

Mama,
Put on my
tennis shoes?
Why? Will we
have to run?

Any More

That day, it all started
because Mama swore
that she had found lipstick
on a shirt Daddy wore

For days, Daddy said
he'd been trying to ignore
a cuff link he had found
on their bedroom floor

They started to fight
Each other's clothes they tore
Daddy hit Mama so hard
She said her jaw was sore

Then he picked up a knife
and his gun from the drawer
like he couldn't decide
which one, either or

He wouldn't stop, the police came
handcuffing him was a chore
Daddy's face was all bloody
and his hands they did gore

Since Mama's been dead
Granny's tears they down pour
My Daddy's been in jail
since I was four

And even though things weren't
that good before
It just doesn't feel
like a family any more

Another Mother

I want another mother
the little girl said
I just wish my
real mother was dead
No I'm not crazy!
I'm not sick in the head!
You all need to be
examining her instead

Let her tell you why
last night I fled,
and why going back
home tonight, I dread.
She beat me for eating
a stale piece of bread
and then made sure that
her boyfriend was fed

Then she grabbed me and
into my dark room she led
She tied me up and told
me my legs to spread
She let her nasty boyfriend
crawl up in my bed
and when I screamed she hit
me with a pipe made of lead.

She said if I told on
her new guy named Fred,
She would sew up my lips
with needle and thread
That's why I slit my wrists
I forgot blood was so red
And that's why I wish
she was dead!

Extra Ordinary

You've got
to be
Extra ordinary
to survive
These days

But you
can be
exceptional
in so
many ways

Whether you
are a
boy or a girl
Here's what to do to
make it in this world

Try not
accepting it
if someone says you cannot
by telling them politely
"You've underestimated me a lot"

Try being
more honest
having more self esteem
Caring more for one another
reaching more for your dream

Try proving
to yourself that
you are a little stronger
By thinking a little smarter
and studying a little longer

Try having
a little more drive
and more determination
Not stopping until you've
had more and more education

Try putting
Him first in
all you do and say
Praising His holy name
Each time you pray

It takes
being extra ordinary
and yes this is a test
Believe more in yourself
and no one can deny you success!!!

The Shallow End

We watch our little children
As they impatiently begin
To enter Life's waters
at the shallow end.
We know that upon us
They entirely depend
for all their protection
and their needs to attend.

But look at all the things
that on money we spend,
So that our children can
Keep up with the latest trend
We do this over and
sometimes over again.
We cripple our children
and some never learn to swim

We stumbled, remember how?
and took it on the chin
But all our children see
is how much we pretend.
The solution to this problem
is so simple, it's a sin
We take a little from the old days
Mix with today and blend

Make some constant rules
and never let them bend
Let them earn their money
and not expect for us to lend.
For all our love and kindness
We cannot possibly defend
If our children get trapped
in Life's shallow end.

"The Marshalling"

Chapter Two

"The Starting Line"

The Parade...

...Teen girls worry
about this and that
if they are too tall
or if they are too fat

And they worry constantly
'Bout makin' a passin' grade
But Life ain't nothin' but
a Parade

Sometimes you get to ride
in Life, sometimes you have to walk
Sometimes you must stand behind
the line drawn with chalk

In the midst of the excitment
things sometimes get delayed
But Life ain't nothin' but
a Parade...

You Are Poetry

You are poetry
You are song
As a child of
God's universe
You do belong

You are poetry
You are rhyme
See how
carefully you can
manipulate Time

You are poetry
You are prose
Hear how each
word's place
it knows

You are poetry
You are verse
Taste each word
as it comes
out to nurse

You are poetry
You are love
smell your
bouquet of
ideas from above

You are poetry
You are song
Feel the pulse
of your meter
Oh so strong

You are poetry!

Not What I Heard

You say you're sorry
for what you did
well don't tell me
Try telling your kid

You said you'd quit lying
You gave her your word
and besides
that's not what I heard

You say you did
not mean to shock her
with the news you just
found out from the doctor

What you're saying
to me sounds absurd
and besides
that's not what I heard

You know you been shooting up
with your boys wearing braids
and now thanks to you
her Mama's got AIDS

I guess now all your little girl's
dreams get deferred
and besides
that's just what I heard

Annie's Baby

Remember me?
I'm the welfare lady
who took the first report
on you and your baby
I've gotten more complaints
I get one daily
so I decided to see
If something is shady

Annie, Chile, where do
you think you're going?
And who's that old man
out there blowing?
Chile you need to
change your plan
You don't need to be
with that old man

You're just thirteen
Not even grown
So why are you trying
to be on your own
And tell me where's the baby
like I asked you before
You think your mama's got him?
Try next door?

Excuse me ma'am
Do you have Annie's baby
He is your grandchild!
Want him to grow up crazy?
Who's got the baby?
Before you sniff up any more
You think the Daddy's got
the baby? Try next door?

Excuse me Mister Brown
Do you have Annie's baby?
You are the father!
Well okay, maybe
Say your girl friend threw
him up against the wall?
Said it woke you up
when you heard him fall?

He was crying, she went off
when he would't stop?
When your girl gets to drinking,
she can't take noise a lot?
I can see Sir that
your mind's a little hazy
Said the ambulance took him?
Said he was breathing lazy?

Doctor, how's the baby
He took his last breath?
The diagnosis?
Beaten to death?
YYYes I knew the situation
NNNo I am not lazy
I just spent all day
LLLooking for that baby

How long have I had the case?
WWWWWell, YYYYYes SSSir, MMMaybe
I probably should have
taken Annie's baby

The Same Boy

I didn't mean
to hurt you
I'm sorry I
ran away

But I was
tired of
hearing 'bout
"back in your day"

You always
acted like
you, I would
annoy

And I just
wanted to
find me a
little joy

I just wanted
you to find
some time
for me

If something
happened
to see if
you would worry

I hated seeing
you painted
up and acting
so coy

While different
men treated
you like their
dog's little toy

You called me names
I never heard
when you caught us
"doing the do"

But if I am all
those things
then Mama,
what are you?

Yeah, we had Kool-Aid, sex,
and a bag of Chips AHoy
But Mama, at least
I was with the same boy!

All Over

Used to be a time
when you said I
was all you need

Used to be a time
that to get to me
you would speed

Used to be a time
when you would call me
if you were free

Used to be a time
when your hands were
ALL OVER me

My friends told me that
I better think
about it twice

My friends told me that
You were always
way too nice

My friends told me that
you and some girl been
out riding around

My friends told me that
they have seen you two
ALL OVER town

I just want to say
If I find out that
this is true

I just want to say
exactly what I'll
do to you

I just want to say
this calmly, trying
not to cuss

I just want to say
It's ALL OVER
between us!!!

Poetry to Me

It lets
me play with Time
to satisfy
my mind
It fills
a place inside
with a joy
I cannot hide

It allows
me to be
anyone
I see
It forces
me to change
and my world
to rearrange

It permits
me with brevity
to add a
little levity
It softens
my tears
and calms all
my fears

It makes
me glad
when I have
been sad
In a way
I've never told
It dances
with my soul

"The Starting Line"

Chapter Three

"The Barricades"

The Parade...

...Teen boys worry
about havin' friends
and havin' on the right pair
of expensive gyms

Sometimes all they think about
is when they will get laid
Good thing Life is only
a Parade

You can be out marchin'
or on the sidelines cheerin'
You can be ridin' on a float
or be the one that's steerin'

You might even have to figure out
Your way around a blockade
But Life is only
a Parade

Second Chance

You've screwed up time
and time again
Taking short cuts
Bettin' you could win

You should feel so grateful
you could almost prance
'Cause God gave you
a second chance

You should not have denied it
the way that you did
Turned out she was not really
pregnant with your kid

So I'll excuse you while
you whirl and dance
You got you
a second chance

You almost went to prison
Copped a plea like before
I'm tired of your line
about being so "pore"

So you're walkin' 'round broke
not a dime in your pants
But what you've got is
a second chance

Always tryin' to be liked,
tryin' to impress everyone
There was none of you left
when all was said and done

It's like all your life
You've been in a trance
But you still got
a second chance

You have just got
to love yourself first
No tellin' what would have
happened if you got any worse

Get a better life now
Give Education a dance
'Cause you've been given
a second chance

Always try to be the
best you can be
This is your only option
Can't you see

So against drugs and violence
You must take a stance
and thank God for
your second chance

Pay Some Dues

Turn off the TV
You ain't watching no news
If you live in my house
You will hear my views

To have a steady job
You do not choose
But you always want a
new pair of shoes

You don't believe
in sitting in any pews
You think Life has a
control called "Cruise"

Well, I know some
drugs you have used
And I know you
like to drink up my booze

But each time you gamble
You will always lose
And you will always be
singing the blues

The secret to success
You have no clues
Son, there is no "Free Lunch"
You got to pay some dues!!!!!!

How Could I?

How could I
have told you,
How much I
want to hold you,

and thought
of you so much
when we have never
even touched?

How could I
have missed you
When I have never
even kissed you

and let you
break my heart
and let us
be far apart?

How could I
forget you
When I've never
even met you

And be
such a fool
For the new
girl in school?

How could I?

No Labels

I bet you like
to watch TV on cable
and dream of
owning a real sable
Don't we all?

Wishing's a ball

So why'd you turn
my life into a fable
That simply
will not enable
Me to grow

You didn't know?

What if I suddenly
turned the table
and lumped you
into a stable
With anyone?

Wouldn't be much fun

Then why'd you
give me a "LABEL"
Since then no one
has been able
To see me

I wish I was free!

"Bone"

I need to tell you
about this young boy named "Bone"
To whom I'll always be grateful
to me, the ropes he has shown

He was the most popular boy
I had ever known
With his two beepers
and his cellular phone

He would laugh and clown with us
and Man could he "jone"
But when it came to business
You would think he was grown

I liked the way
he was never alone
Always had "his boys"
around him in a zone

After he got himself set
His clothes he had sewn
Quickly built him an empire
and did it all on his own

He owned six cars
and a beautiful home
and at his funeral
his family did moan

On his expensive
marble head stone reads
"Here lies sixteen year old
Bad to the Bone"

In Your Face

Each time Michael got the ball
At least five other men gave chase
Some of his team mates were even
jealous of his ability and grace

He knew someone would try to stop him
If they had to hang off of his waist
But Michael would spin, slam dunk the ball
and signal, "IN YOUR FACE!"

Michael would do his best
even if he was wearing a brace
He never followed the crowd
He moved at his own pace

You see, he's full of pride from
his bald head to his shoe lace
His Three-pointer would fall, all net
and he'd motion, "IN YOUR FACE!"

You don't have to be just like Mike
Do your best in any case
Study real hard in school
You have no time to waste

Want to do something so badly
the victory you can taste
When you're told you can't, JUST DO IT!
Then signal, "IN YOUR FACE!!!!!!!"

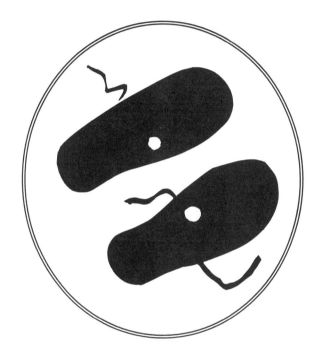

"The Barricades"

Chapter Four

"The Procession"

The Parade...

...Single women worry
"bout their figures and their hair
Havin' a career and someone
who will really care

And rushing off to work
leavin' the bed unmade
But remember, Life is only
a Parade

You cannot see what's to come in Life
only from where you begin
and there might be somethin' better
that is comin' 'round the bend

So feel good 'bout yourself
without gettin' it okayed
"Cause Life sho' ain't nothin' but
a Parade

The Horizontal Position

You can call me strange
But I believe this superstition
In all my fifty years
I ain't seen no contradiction

Now you can put this in print
I mean the final edition
Don't believe nothin' a man says
in the Horizontal Position

You can stop all that laughin'
I ain't heard no opposition
You ladies know what I mean
We should sign a petition

I mean it's a rite of passage
like a custom, a tradition
You can't believe nothin' a man whispers
in the Horizontal Position

Now if you find out I'm lying
I'd be the first to make an admission
This is so incredible
it defies description

I am telling you the God's honest truth
that should take away suspicion
Don't believe a word a man utters
in the Horizontal Position

Now I know the menfolk gon' cuss
They probably checkin' their ammunition
But we women got to stick together
I don't care the weather condition

Now you know we should stand up
and exercise our will and volition
But beware of every single word he moans
in the Horizontal Position

I know I got's my facts straight
Naw! This ain't no rendition
and my customers will back me up
Cause you see, I am a beautition

We gots to stop lettin' these
men talk us into submission
Don't believe nothin' he grunts
in the Horizontal Position

If just once you can prove me wrong
I will pay you a commission
But I'd have to check him out
Make sure he ain't no apparition

If you could find one honest man
He would be a welcome addition
But don't believe nothing he screams
in the Horizontal Position

Love Waitin'

Don't you think
That man's a little old
for you to be datin'
I know you think
I'm crazy, but my thoughts
I am a statin'

If he ain't thinkin' 'bout
what you thinkin' 'bout
Don't you try no manipulatin'
Chile, if you don't watch out
a fine mess you'll be creatin'

'Fore you say you in love
both of ya'll must
be participatin'
Naw, I ain't gonna shut up
Even if my naggin'
is irritatin'

I been watchin' you
for three months now
And a baby you may be creatin'
What you gon' do
When it backfires
That love trap you been baitin'

What's the matter with you, Chile?
We can hear your
cries resonatin'
I know exactly how it hurts
when you thought you had
some love waitin'

I tried my best
to convince you he wasn't
thinkin' 'bout no obligatin'
I know you feel your life's
over, but the world's
gonna keep rotatin'

You askin' how could he
mistreat you, when it was
your miscalculatin'
Chile, don't you know
that with love their can
be no imitatin'

You know all men
are not dogs, so you can
stop your insinuatin'
Even animals got sense
enough to wait 'til
they hear a call for matin'

Your constant whinin'
and cryin' on my nerves
it is gratin'
Your life has got to go on
Your feelings you can
start uncratin'

Now your son didn't ask
to be born, so ain't no need
of him you hatin'
Come on and bring that
Chile to Granny 'cause
I gots him some love waitin'

My Eyes

Through my 17
year old eyes
He looked so handsome
and seemed so wise
I didn't know it was
all a disguise
for my 17
year old eyes

Through my 21
year old eyes
blurred with the
tears of the Whys?
I didn't know love
could be all lies
in front of my 21
year old eyes

Through my 25
year old eyes
The mirror's reflection
I still despise
I didn't know how
it'd feel when love dies
before my 25
year old eyes

Through my 30
year old eyes
greeting the day
after several tries
I didn't know how
fast time flies
past my 30
year old eyes

Through my 35
year old eyes
I caught the brief beauty
of a new sun rise
I didn't know Life
without the sighs
Through my 35
year old eyes

Through my 40
year old eyes
To Despair I have
said my goodbyes
I didn't know Life
had wonder and surprise
for my 40
year old eyes

Through my 45
year old eyes
I stopped eating all
those cakes and pies
And started trimming down
these old thighs
for my 45
year old eyes

Through my 50
year old eyes
I thank God for
each day I arise
To love me
is the real prize
for my 50
year old eyes

Since We Met

After so many nights
with my pillow case wet
A survivor of love wars
I am a vet

On finding someone real
I had my heart set
This would never happen
I used to fret

Sad and Lonely
would aid and abet
Pitiful and Angry
in this familiar quartet

Being alone so long
Common sense you forget
and you can find yourself
staring at the gas jet

But I don't worry any more
about being in debt
Folks on my job
can't get me upset

Because my dear
ever since we met
Better than this
It does not get

In all my life
I have but one regret
That we didn't
meet sooner, but yet

I'm thanking My God
on this you can bet
Allowing me to escape
Lonely's tight net

I don't need a mink
I don't need a corvette
Now that my life is more
than just feeding my pet

Because sweetheart,
ever since we met
This is as good
as it can get

In Love Again

I don't know about you
I was 'bout to swear off all men
But I decided to give
that ole bottle one more spin

And Chile, I ain't been wearin'
Nothin' but this grin
Sister girl, I'm tryin' to tell you
I'm back in love again

You don't need to go notify
my very next of kin
I know what I am doing
to my business, I can tend

Chile, I'll know just what to do
If this time I win
But for now it feels good
to be back in love again

Okay, I'll slow down and try
not to smother him
I know that over backwards
I usually bend

But Chile, did you see that dimple
in the middle of his chin
and Girl, I'm back,
Back in love again!

Down Love's blind alleys
I know that I have been
Don't keep reminding me
just try to be my friend

I pray each and every day
That this love won't end
But Wheeeeeee!!!" Look at me!
I'm back in love again

Yeah I remember my bad luck
No this ain't my trend
But let me wear your diamond earrings
and your diamond stick pin?

If I fall down, I promise
I will take it on the chin
But for now Friend girl
I'm back in love again!!!!!

To Love Someone

To love someone
is a responsibility
and not one to take
lightly

To love someone
is more than a kiss
or just holding someone
tightly

To love someone
is to want them
even when they look
unsightly

To love someone
is to color their day
all warmly and
brightly

To love someone
is to be there for them
wrongly or
rightly

To love someone
is to handle their
feelings and fears
politely

To love someone
is to express it
somehow, daily and
nightly

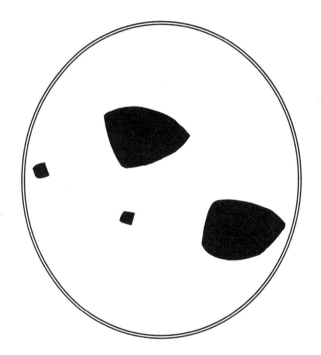

"The Procession"

Chapter Five

"The Clowns"

The Parade...

...Single Men worry
'Bout tryin' to impress,
the correct wine to drink,
Lookin' the part of success

And doin' just enough work
to keep on gettin' paid
They know Life ain't nothin' but
a Parade

Sometimes balloons burst or fly away
and the twirling baton hits the ground
Sometimes when you pass by
the crowd will not make a sound

Sometimes you have to play the clown
to avoid the next tirade
Just remember, Life is only
a Parade...

More or Less

I must admit
I have to confess
That this must be
some kind of test

I feel like a pawn
in a game of chess
What do you want?
I cannot guess

Your toying with me
I think is grotesque
Especially when our life
could have been picturesque

If I knew how, I would
make a Citizen's arrest
I don't know if I can take
much more of this stress

I trusted you
with my openness
I gave more and more
I saw you less and less

Now around my heart I have
built a fortress
While you're walking around
with your stuck out chest

I may never find
any happiness
But to see you once more
I couldn't care less!

The Word Go

There was this girl I wanted
to impress and to show
So my friends convinced me
on a date we should go

So I cleaned up my crib
put the chairs in a neat row,
cut my hair and shaved,
tied my tie in a bow

I changed the bulbs to give
the room a soft glow
I'd have gotten some chips
but my money was low

Everything was so smooth
and my courage did grow
I tried to ask her for some
and she screamed OH NO!

Then she laughed at me,
said she thought I was slow
That wounded my pride
you know the male ego

So I told her "forget the weave"
just let her hair grow
She tried to kick me
and stumped her big toe

Then I jumped on her back
and said "Giddy up, Whoa!"
I guess I was wrong
from the word go

I Can't Dance

Look like you haven't
slept in days
How does she put
up with your stupid ways
Look like you in
some kinda trance
Naw Man, I just
can't dance

How long, like this,
you been strung out
You don't know what
this is all about?
They want to arrest you,
I'm your last chance?
Naw, Man, I really
can't dance

Ooh, your ole girl's
gonna curse
You stole her bank card
from her purse
You couldn't get no
cash advance
Naw, Bro, I still
can't dance

You always want
money from me
Like I'm some
kinda money tree
I don't care what's
your circumstance
Man, I just
can't dance!!!

Was That Goodbye

I'll admit I didn't
quite understand
What to do, to prove
that I was your man

Then you said that without me
You thought you would die
as you spilled some soup
on my favorite silk tie

Then you touched my face
and said "my...my...my"
As you ordered a hamburger
with an extra fry

Then you said you loved me
and made a deep sigh,
As you sat there eating
my sweet potato pie

Then you said you wanted me
to keep my self respect
and insisted I finally pay
for a luncheon check

Then you said that there
was nothing left to say,
You left me standing there
got in your Benz, and drove away

Tell me was everything
you said to me a lie?
Did I miss something
or was that Good-bye?

Someone Believes

When someone believes
in you
the toughest times you can get through
There's nothing you
cannot do
When someone believes in you

When someone tells you
that you can
and respect you begin to demand
There's nothing you
cannnot understand
When someone tells you that you can

When someone wants
to validate you
and reminds you God did create you
There's no one who
can berate you
When someone wants to validate you

When someone loves you
as a friend
and stays through thick and thin
There's no battle you
cannot win
When someone loves you as a friend

When someone holds you
in prayer
and you know they really do care
There's no burden you
cannot bear
When someone holds you in prayer

When someone knows you've
been anointed
So a nose becomes disjointed
There's no way to
become disappointed
When someone knows you're anointed

When someone knows
you inside
God's plan for you cannot be denied
There's no talent He will
let you hide
When someone knows you inside

When someone believes
in you
Be that light for someone else too
There is no way to forget
to say "Thank You"
When someone believes in you

Not Now

When you ask God a question
He answers the only way
He knows how
I don't care what your
prayer is, He says
Yes, No, or Not Now

When God answers Yes!,
It doesn't matter
what you do
It will turn out all right
The Lord can really
come through

And when He says No!,
You can try with
all your might
I don't care how smart
you are, nothing
will turn out right

When it seems like
He didn't give you something
you thought you had earned,
It means He's trying to tell you
there is something else
you need to learn

And when you want a
silk purse from the
ear of a sow
God is always listening
He's just saying Not now

"The Clowns"

Chapter Six

"The Reviewing Stand"

The Parade...

...Married women worry
'bout the job and family jugglin'
and findin' a fraction of time
when they can stop their strugglin'

Tryin' to cook breakfast
while their chile's hair they braid
You're right, Life Ain't nothin' but
a Parade

You must pass the reviewin' stand
and get checked out by the judges
You can be doing all you can
and they may still hold grudges

Sometimes the silence is so deafening
Your nerves can get very frayed
But remember Life ain't nothin' but
a Parade...

The Black Woman's Book

Individual as each flake of snow
As Black women our lives intertwine so
In a faded dress
Waiting on the sun
In the Black woman's book
Poor is Chapter One

A Need that will not sit still
A Want ready to explode or kill
A growing anger
that is not new
In the Black woman's book
Hard is Chapter Two

Too much, too soon, too often again
No disgust, no fighting,
no arguing, will win
In the Black woman's book
Chapter Three
Is all about Responsibility

Wounded, still with children to protect
Seated amidst the notices of disconnect
Tears passing each other
As they race to the floor
In the Black woman's book
Alone is Chapter Four

Trying to hold on while taking Life's curves
Just getting rebalanced and again
having to swerve
In the Black woman's book
Chapter Five is all about
Just staying alive

With demands forcing the back
into an awkward arch
Everyone else has their tune for us to march
Other's broken dreams
We are trying to fix
In the Black woman's book
Selfless is Chapter Six

Guided by a belief in things not seen
and having only God
on whom we can lean
Needing to know there is a Heaven
In the Black woman's book
Spirituality is Chapter Seven

Fighting for the right to be alright,
then finding the way when
the path is void of light
Being prepared, but having to wait
In the Black woman's book
Difficult is Chapter Eight

Mirroring the image
of an accurate reflection
and loving it after introspection
Untying all the ties that bind
In the Black woman's book
Self-love is Chapter Nine

But, no mole hill, no man, and no mountain
can stop the creativity of our flowing fountain
Bring on Impossible
We are ready to begin
Because in the Black woman's book
Determination is Chapter Ten!

For Me

I must admit I'm quite puzzled
and would really like to know

Why are you still here?
I told you, you had to go

If you are here for how I look,
I find nothing queerer

You have spent every minute of
this marriage looking in the mirror

If you are here 'cause my home is pretty,
I really must beg your pardon

You need to get a subscription
to Better Homes and Garden

If you are here for how I dress
and not for what I know,

You need to try and get some tickets
to the Ebony Fashion show

If you're here 'cause my cooking
is as good as it can be,

You need to get you a date
with that woman named Sara Lee

And if you are here 'cause my pay check
is more and yours is always less,

You need to get you a Gold Card
from American Express

I admit I work very hard
I'm too tired to really care

So, why are you still here?
You're not going anywhere?

If you are here for material things
and not for who you see,

We can't stay married any longer,
Unless you love me for me!

You Are Loved

As a lit candle firmly
chases away the darkness,
You are loved

Like a baby's first cry
pierces the air,
You are loved

As a rosebud gradually opens
to a mature flower,
You are loved

Like a mountain proudly
shelters the valley,
You are loved

As the waters undulate to
caress the shore,
You are loved

Like Time alternates between
racing and standing still
You are loved

As the night faithfully
kisses the dawn,
You are loved

Like an eagle steadily soars
to heights before unseen
You are loved

You are loved
You are loved...

The Invitation

The invitation was into your love
I thought
So three children into the marriage
I brought

I soon realized up in your pain we
were caught
Not seeing it sooner, a lesson I
was taught

For years all your selfish lies
I bought
I regret that in front of my children
we fought

Trying to get you to get help was all
for naught
Each night's been sleepless, with tears
been wraught

Every moment with you, with peril has
been fraught
For what you've done to us, feeling hatred
I ought

But for now I have no time to feel
distraught
Because refuge from you, tonight we
have sought

Today

Somebody tried to mess with me
Today
They tried to take all my joy
away
The reason only Jealousy can say
Somebody tried to mess with me
Today

Somebody tried to hurt me
Today
And then evil vibes they tried
to spray
The reason only Envy can say
Somebody tried to hurt me
Today

Somebody tried to abuse me
Today
Take my Time and Talent
without pay
The reason only Sexism can say
Somebody tried to abuse me
Today

Somebody tried to stop me
Today
Put me in "my place"
and make me stay
The reason only Racism can say
Somebody tried to stop me
Today

Whoever tried to mess with me
Today
Your life is full of rot and decay
The reason only Low Self Esteem can say
Whoever tried to mess with me
Today!

Whoever tried to hurt me
Today
To be forgiven, you better pray
The reason only Time can say
Whoever tried to hurt me
Today!!

Whoever tried to abuse me
Today
Just caused more blessings to come my way
The reason only Justice can say
Whoever tried to abuse me
Today!!!

Whoever tried to stop me
Today
You will surely have Hell to pay
The reason only God can say
Whoever tried to stop me
Today!!!!

The Sistership

Ten fine black sisters sat at lunch
Looking as good as they wanted

Charting a stormy business course
Proceeding ahead undaunted

Sharing ideas and pain, pain and ideas
As their drinks they slowly sipped

They had come from all across the
country for this Washington D.C. trip

Each dressed in a power suit
with beautiful fashion clips

They had just left the White House
Hearing the President say "Read my Lips"

Munching on raw vegetables
with a creamy low calorie dip

Joking about how it feels to be
the cookie's only chocolate chip

It really was not that long ago
from our homeland we were ripped

And our forefathers backs bore the
brunt of the leather whip

They left emotionally full and satisfied
after splitting the check and tip

Why was what they shared so rare?
This thing called Black Sistership

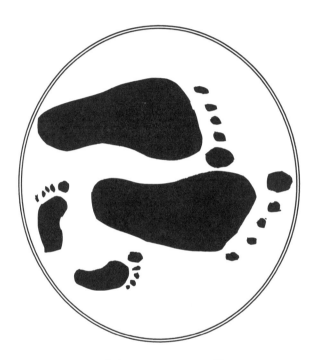

"The Reviewing Stand"

Chapter Seven

"The Party"

The Parade...

...Married men worry
'Bout their next vacation
and payin' all the bills
in their monthly rotation

Patchin' up places on the house
where the wood has decayed
Gee! Life ain't nothin' but
a Parade

Sometimes your hopes get cancelled
or rescheduled altogether,
but you must perform your best
in any kind of weather

So find your own spot in Life
and don't get so dismayed
'Cause Life ain't nothin' but
a Parade...

A Dollar Short

I don't like to talk about
nobody
Especially not about my mate
But after getting to know
his family
It must be some kind of trait

I noticed this annoying
habit
on our very first date
Took me awhile
to realize
this was a permanent state

He didn't order anything
then reached
over for my plate
When they brought
the check
He said we might have to wait

I thought he was joking
when he asked about
the dishwashing rate
He said I shouldn't mind,
It was
because of him I ate

You know this kind of person
The kind
I really hate
The one who's always
a dollar short and
always a day late

While I'm Ahead

Sweet heart, I need to confess
and this is
something that I dread

About the time
I stole our
neighbor's loaf of bread

That was me who
sewed your pockets
with needle and thread

and about the time
I painted
your Sunday shoes red

and about the time
I used ketchup
and pretended that I bled

Or when I slipped
out to a party
and you thought I was in bed

I just had to confess
on this day
before we rewed

But I think I
better quit
while I'm ahead

Windows of Time

We held on
so tightly
because we didn't know
What would happen if
we let each other go

But we must
live out our lives
in windows of time
When the window is closed
we must put up a sign

When the
window is open
we each must obey
rules of the unspoken
game we play

As the
window closes again
we each must remind
the other of their
commitments of time

We don't
know what we mean
to one another
We just turn out the lights
and climb under the cover

There is
havoc created
in our minds
when our windows are not
open at the same time

The only
trouble with
playing this game
Is we're not ever sure
of anything but our name

Our relationship
must always
remain ill defined
Because all we have
are brief windows of time

You Are My Friend

You make me laugh at my mistakes
You make me give whatever it takes

You make me feel I can stand alone
You make me know that I can phone

You make me know just where to begin
You are my friend

You can always lift my spirit
You can tell if I don't want to hear it

You can be glad if I win the prize
You can always bring me down to size

You can make me feel that I can win
You are my friend

You let me cry like a child
You let me know I am worthwhile

You let me forget all my woes
You let me stay sharp on my toes

You let me see what's around the bend
You are my friend

You help me fix my broken dreams
You help me figure out what Life means

You help make my load a little lighter
You help make my day a little brighter

You help me realize how blessed I've been
Because you are my friend

The Dreamer

It wasn't until she
had broken my femur

That I realized she
was gettin' meaner

Up against the wall, she
threw the coffee creamer

Said that she couldn't keep
the house any cleaner

Then she burned me, with
an electric rice steamer

At her birthday party she
set fire to a streamer

She first became a hustler
and then a schemer

I finally realized
that I married a dreamer

Then she became a maniac
and a constant screamer

She got worse and worse
as times got leaner

I pray that the Lord
will be my redeemer

But I just didn't know
that I had married a dreamer

But A Wheel

Be careful how
you make me feel
One day I might have
to give you a meal
And find a way
to honestly deal
'Cause Life ain't
nothin' but a wheel

To rumor and gossip
your lips you can seal
Try spending your time
on things that are real
And you should not cheat,
lie or steal
'Cause Life ain't
nothin' but a wheel

Don't step on someone
with your heel
One day your fate
they may have to seal
From the boomerang effect
you may reel
'Cause Life ain't
nothin' but a wheel

Let all of us
begin to heal
Live our lives
with zest and zeal
But we cannot
forget to kneel
'Cause Life ain't
nothin' but a wheel

"The Party"

Chapter Eight

"The Dispersal"

The Parade...

...Elderly people worry
'Bout their Social Security check
living Life with dignity and
holding on to their self respect

And constantly being shunned
just because they have grayed
But they know Life is only
a Parade

Some people don't stay 'til the end
to see how it all turns out
You may not get noticed
even if you scream and shout

But you'll want more and more
attention, with each passing decade
'Cause Life ain't nothin' but
a Parade...

70 Somethin'

I'm seventy today
and I feel okay
Well, I'm seventy-one
and still a whole lot of fun
I'm seventy-two
and I'm through with you
Chile, I'm seventy-three
and as cute as can be
I'm seventy-four
Got more living in store
Ain't we somethin'
Ain't we somethin'

Shoot! I'm seventy-five
and still alive
Well, I'm seventy-six
you better watch your tricks
I'm seventy-seven
gettin' ready for heaven
Chile, I'm seventy-eight
and goin' out on a date
Hell! I'm seventy-nine
and I'm still so fine
Ain't we somethin'
Ain't we somethin'

We seventy-somethin'
our hearts are still pumpin'
Last night, dressed up
We had the joint jumpin'
We can't take a whole lot
of shoving and bumpin'
But we seventy-plus and

Ain't we somethin'!!!!!!
Ain't we somethin'!!!!!!

'Round Here

Things just don't smell right
'round here
I miss my honey suckle
near the fence
Ever since my grandson came to stay
all I smell is his stankin' incense

Things just don't taste right
'round here
I'm too nervous to eat a bite
Ever since my grandson came to stay
I have lost my appetite

Things just don't sound right
'round here
I can hear all this slammin'
Ever since my grandson came to stay
Strange people, at my door be bammin'

Things just don't feel right
'round here
Everythin' I'm startin' to despise
Ever since my grandson came to stay
all he tells me is a bunch of lies

Things just don't look right
'round here
My TV and stereo are gone
Ever since my grandson came to stay
Everythin' has just gon' wrong

Death

Death makes us
Stop
and find all the
Time
We could never
seem to find
before

Death makes us
Stop
and pay close
Attention
to little things
we used to
ignore

Death makes us
Stop
and say kind
Things
to the ones
we truly
adore

Death makes us
Stop
Cherish family and
friends
and Praise God
Even more

Death makes us
Stop

I Have Lost Someone

I have lost someone
who loved beautiful things
Fragrances and clothes
Jewelry and rings

I have lost someone
who was fun to be with
and whose hearty laughter
was like a precious gift

I have lost someone
active in her community
Whose hope for the world
was for Peace and Unity

I have lost someone
who would tell no lies
about the pain and the sadness
you could see in her eyes

I have lost someone
who searched for peace of mind
An inner peace, while living
she could never find

I have lost someone
whose worth cannot be measured
and each memory of her
will always be treasured

I have lost someone
but I feel no pain
Because I know that my loss
is God's gain

I Miss You

My head has stopped all
learning
My senses are not
returning
Money, I don't feel like
earning
I miss you

My eyes, looking for you keep
turning
My heart has a constant
burning
My stomach is always
churning
I miss you

My decisions I keep
overturning
My sensibilities I must start
relearning
My love, for you I am still
yearning
I miss you

Like a Mountain

One day I saw a mountain
whispering to a cloud
It's thoughts of peace and love
it could never say out loud

And I thought how wonderful
it must be to be like a cloud
floating up in the air
able to whisper to mountains

The next day I returned
and the cloud had scampered away
but the mountain was standing as proud
as it had been the other day

Majestic and proud
not because of its beauty
but providing shelter to those
in Life's valley as its duty

And I thought how magnificent
it must be to be like a mountain
feet on the ground
but able to whisper to clouds

The Parade...

...For the days you wished
that in bed you had stayed

For the times, your thoughts
someone tried to invade

For the days your ideas
were not properly conveyed

For the times you wished that
it was less that you weighed

For the days you needed
emotional first aid

For the times you wanted
someone else's life in trade

For the days someone tried
your work to degrade

For the times and things
about which you prayed

Just relax a bit
and go find some shade
And get a cool drink of
some fresh lemonade
Believe it or not
You have really
got it made
Remember, Life ain't nothin' but
a Parade!!!!!!!!!!!!!!!!!!!!!!!